A great figure or physique is nice, but it's self-confidence that makes someone really sexy.

ALTOKI

22

albacar
JCV

MONAJ
EMPRESA
SLX

asesores de navarra
asesores de navarra

64
70
GRAN VIA

IDC
MONAJ

latexco
vermarc
UCI
TEAM TIME TRIAL
WORLD CHAMPIONS
latexco
QUICK·STE
FLOORS

TOULOUSE
206
kiwami

204
203

456
458

CCSU
458
CCSU
456
CCSU
454

POIDS-LOURDS
OUEST
Harmonie mutuelle
Chanoine.fr
SUD DE L'EURE
CYCLISME
Intermarché
HYPER
VERNEUIL SUR-AVRE
Expresso
Service

NJIT
race|result
794
CCSU
race|result
746
CCSU
race|result
747

crivit
PRO

GBR
2XU

SCOTT
CONCEPT
CYCLON

AMBAR
SCOTT
CYCLON
CYCLON

AMBAR
AMBAR
SCOTT
CYCLON
TowCar

CYCLON

DEVRON

Cofidis
3

Michaël D'Almeida

STADIUM
VENECIA
RIDAO
adidas

Cholet

QUICK-STEP
latexco
QUICK-STEP FLOORS
SPECIALIZED
51

КАТЮША
ITERA
OW
RUSkin Suits
www.skinsuits.ru

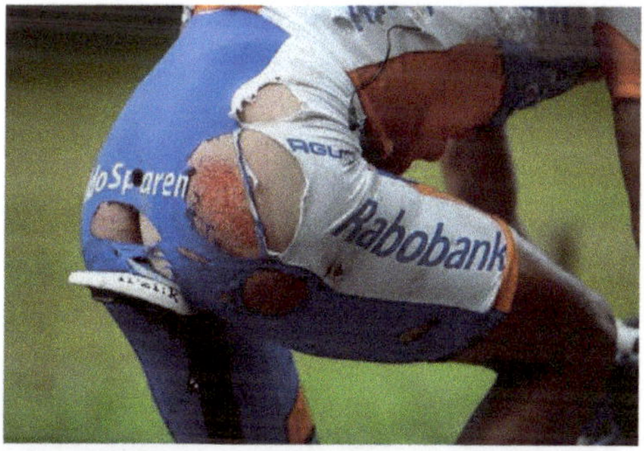
Rabobank

FDJ

Prestigio
SVK
kiwami

sky
SWIFT

le coq sportif
ŠKODA
Deloitte
dimension data
dimension
dimension data

ITALIA
ITALIA

ASTANA
181

Suharzevskis
LAT
SUUNTO
EŽI

LACLASSICA
35

OPOSICIONES
FEMI
17

Cholet

iPad
16:36
20 %

21
FDJ

METALGRAF
SH
METALGRAF
METALGRAF

187
Royal Smilde
Credit Agricole
WALLONIE
BRUXELLES

ALXEN
ALXEN
SALUD DEPORTIVA
KING

SRAM
ROCK
SHOX
Avid
28
28

COLOMA
GOBIK
RITCHEY

CRAFT
CRAFT
TREK

20
73
JUGA
Arbizu
ZM

DEVRON
bellotto

SPECIALIZED
htc
highroad
LEZYNE
25
MOA
highroad

UNIVERSOBIKE
AUTOMOVILES VILLAMAYOR
UNIVERSOBIKE
an-50

AG2R LA
MONDIALE

orca

29
Kalenji
49

WILD
RACE
FINISHER
NAJERA '18

SH
SH

ITERA
GAZPROM
prologo

SUB23 MASCULINO
154

ANTUAN

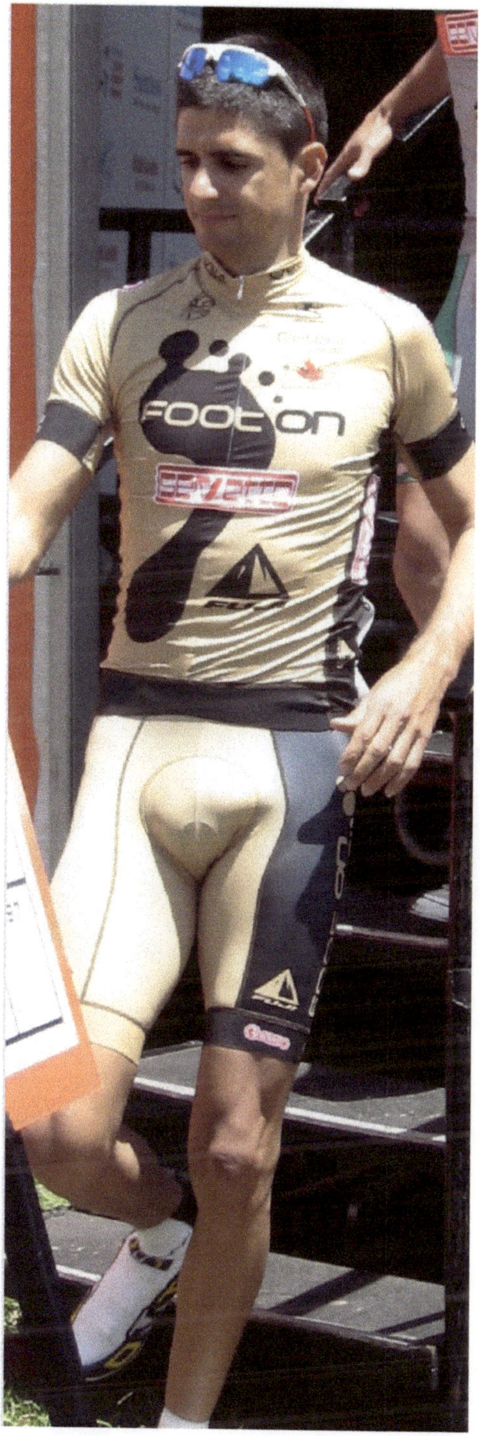
FOOTON

sky
sky
PINARELLO
sky
© Christo

PEUGEOT
etixx
sports nutrition
QUICK-STEP
latexco
LIDL
KBC

BMC

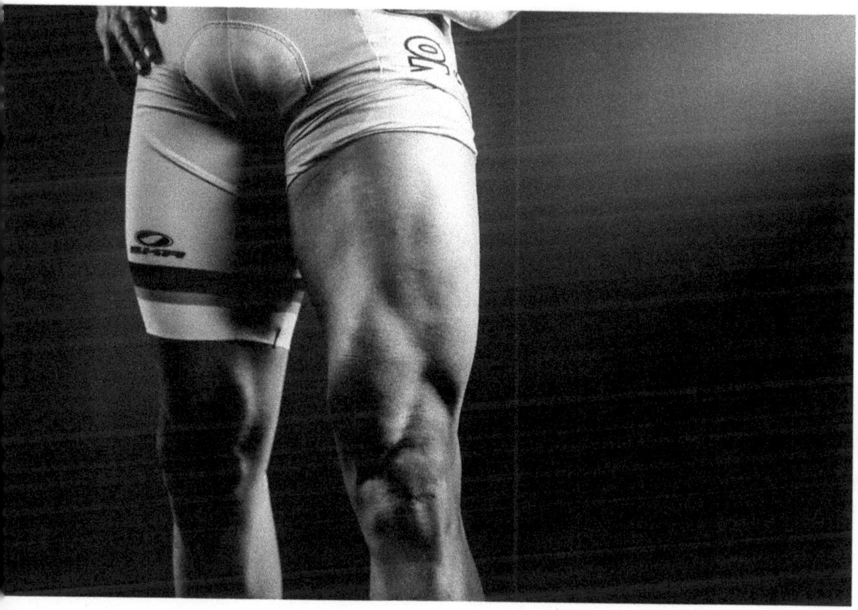

GBR
ESP

SUPERPRESTIGIO
MTB
36
Liberty
Seguros
seguros.pt
ONDA
AERO

LCL
ŠKODA
france•tv sport
Krys
Vittel
QUICK-STEP
FLOORS
QUICK-STEP

BONTRAGER
TREK